HORSES

The LIPIZZAN Horse

by Sarah Maass

Consultant:
Sandy Heaberlin
Director
Lipizzan Association of North America (LANA)
Anderson, Indiana

Capstone press

Mankato, Minnesota

Edge Books are published by Capstone Press,
151 Good Counsel Drive, P.O. Box 669, Mankato, Minnesota 56002.
www.capstonepress.com

Library of Congress Cataloging-in-Publication Data
Maass, Sarah.
    The Lipizzan horse / by Sarah Maass.
    p. cm.—(Edge Books. Horses)
    Summary: "Describes the Lipizzan horse, including its history, physical
features, and uses today"—Provided by publisher.
    Includes bibliographical references (p. 31) and index.
    ISBN-13: 978-0-7368-5459-7 (hardcover)
    ISBN-10: 0-7368-5459-2 (hardcover)
    1. Lipizzaner horse—Juvenile literature. I. Title. II. Series.
SF293.L5M33 2006
636.1'38—dc22   2005017572

Editorial Credits

Carrie A. Braulick, editor; Juliette Peters, set designer; Bobbi J. Dey, book
    designer; Deirdre Barton, photo researcher/photo editor

Photo Credits

1 2 3 4 5 6 11 10 09 08 07 06

Table of Contents

Chapter 1

Great Warhorses

Life was tough for European warhorses during the 1500s. These horses thundered onto battlefields carrying knights. The knights wore heavy metal armor. Mile after mile, warhorses tirelessly carried their heavy loads.

Lipizzan warhorses probably had the hardest jobs of all. Lipizzans were trained to protect their riders. They reared up to shield their riders from enemy weapons. They kicked out their legs to scare away enemy soldiers.

Today, Lipizzans no longer work on battlefields. But people can still see their famous battlefield maneuvers at shows throughout the world.

Learn about:
- ★ Lipizzan ancestors
- ★ The Spanish Riding School
- ★ Lipizzan registries

In the late 1500s, Lipizzans learned their battlefield moves at the Spanish Riding School. Lipizzans continue to train there today.

An Old Breed

The Lipizzan is one of the world's oldest horse breeds. In 1562, Austrian emperor Maximillian II wanted better warhorses. He started a horse breeding farm in Kladrub, Austria. At the farm, he bred Spanish horses with Karst horses. The mix created strong, elegant horses suitable for use in wars.

In 1580, Maximillian's brother Archduke Charles started another horse breeding farm. This farm was located in the small Austrian town of Lipizza. Horse breeders in Lipizza continued crossing Spanish and Karst horses. Over time, the horses from the two farms became known as Lipizzaners, or Lipizzans.

On the Battlefield

Lipizzans learned to be skilled warhorses at the Spanish Riding School in Vienna, Austria. Trainers at the school taught the horses to leap into the air, stand up on their back legs, and kick.

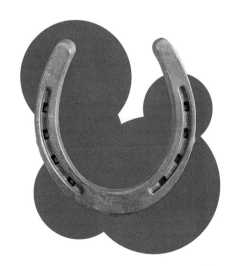

Soon, rulers of other countries wanted the strong, athletic Lipizzans that both scared and amazed them on the battlefield. But Austria's leaders kept their treasured horses to themselves. Only military leaders and members of royalty were allowed to ride them. The royalty often showed off their horses' skills during celebrations.

Lipizzans have been raised at the farm in Lipizza for hundreds of years.

Creating the Modern Lipizzan

The ancestry of Lipizzans remained pure for many years. Lipizzans were not mated with other horse breeds until the late 1700s. Horse breeders then crossed Lipizzans with Neapolitan horses from Italy. Neapolitans gave Lipizzans a fancy, high-stepping trot.

Arabian horses also helped create modern Lipizzans. Some Lipizzans are descendants of Siglavy, a gray Arabian stallion born in 1810.

Lipizzans in the United States

In 1937, Austrian singer Maria Jeritza brought the first Lipizzans to the United States. Eventually, people brought more horses. Between 1958 and 1969, Tempel and Ester Smith brought 37 Lipizzans to the United States.

As time passed, U.S. Lipizzan owners wanted a registry to keep track of their horses' ancestries. In 1969, the Lipizzan Association of America formed. The next year, the United States Lipizzan Registry (USLR) formed. In 1992, the Lipizzan Association of America combined with another group to form the Lipizzan Association of North America (LANA). Together, USLR and LANA have about 1,000 registered horses.

Saving Lipizzans

During World War II (1939–1945), the quick action of an Army general saved Lipizzans from dying out. At the time, only about 500 Lipizzans existed in the world. The stallions were at the Spanish Riding School in Vienna. The mares and foals were in Hostau, Czechoslovakia.

In 1945, the U.S. Army was near Hostau. U.S. General George S. Patton learned the mares and foals were being kept there. To keep the horses safe, he sent a unit of U.S. soldiers to move the horses to Austria. After seeing a performance by the Spanish Riding School, Patton also helped protect the stallions.

◀ George S. Patton

Chapter 2

Super Strength

Capturing attention is easy for Lipizzans. Lipizzans seem to float on air as they move. They hold their heads high and arch their necks. Long, flowing manes and tails add to the Lipizzan's elegance.

Appearance

Lipizzans are shorter than many other breeds. Horses are measured from the ground to the top of their shoulders, or withers. Lipizzans stand between 14.2 and 15.3 hands tall. A hand equals 4 inches (10 centimeters). Many other horses are at least 15 hands tall. An average-sized adult person can see over the back of most Lipizzans.

Learn about:
★ Size
★ Colors
★ A unique Lipizzan trait

The stylish movement of Lipizzans attracts many fans to the breed.

⬆ Lipizzans have muscular necks and shoulders.

FACT

A Lipizzan stallion has a registered name with two parts. One part comes from the father, or sire. The other part comes from the mother, or dam.

What Lipizzans lack in height, they make up for in strength. Lipizzans have wide backs and chests. Their shoulders and necks are muscular. Their hindquarters and back legs are especially strong. Lipizzans use their powerful hindquarters to stand up on their hind legs and do other advanced moves.

Lipizzans have average-sized heads with small, alert ears. Their eyes are large and dark.

▲ Lipizzans have large dark eyes and small ears.

Gray Lipizzan foals keep their dark coats for only a short time.

Color

Almost all Lipizzans are gray. Gray Lipizzans are born black or dark brown. They turn gray over the next few years. The coats of gray Lipizzans then continue to lighten. After about eight years, their coats look white. But their official color is still considered gray.

A few Lipizzans are brown or black. These horses have dark coats throughout their lives.

Personality

When a Lipizzan performs at a show, the rider and horse seem to think as one. The Lipizzan's cooperation and intelligence help create this partnership. Lipizzans learn even the most difficult moves quickly.

They rarely forget what they are taught, even after learning many new moves.

Gentleness rounds out the Lipizzan's personality. Children and beginning riders often are comfortable riding Lipizzans.

Facing Fear

Long ago, horses lived in the wild. Other animals hunted horses. Horses were always aware of their surroundings. They ran from other animals or anything that startled them. Today, most horses still run from things that frighten them. But Lipizzans are different. Training as warhorses taught Lipizzans not to run away. Lipizzans arch their necks and trot in place instead of running away.

◄ Trainers teach Lipizzans to trot in place for shows.

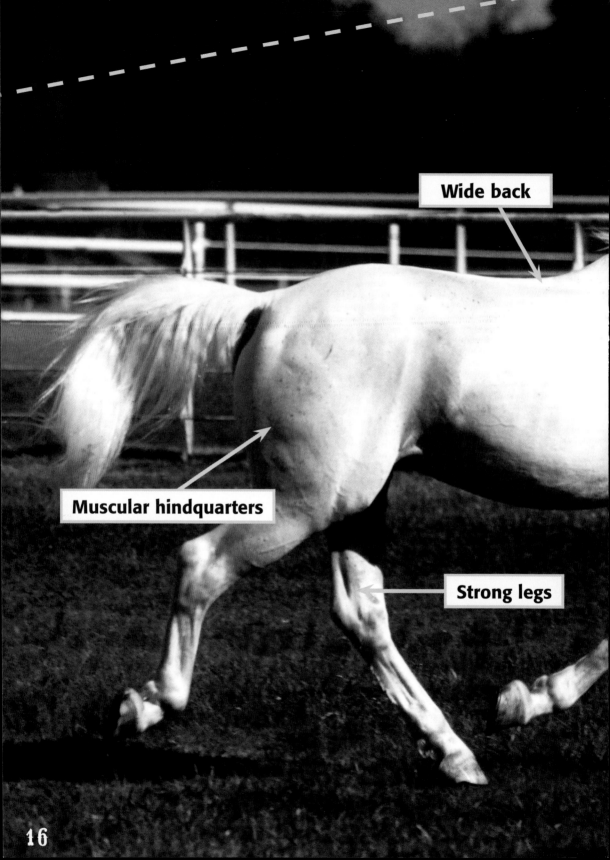

Wide back

Muscular hindquarters

Strong legs

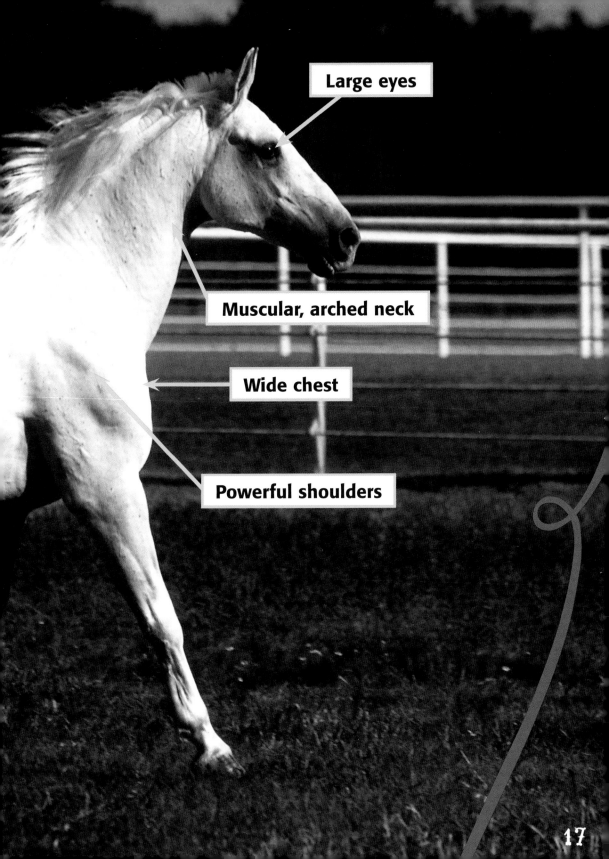

Large eyes

Muscular, arched neck

Wide chest

Powerful shoulders

Chapter 3

Flying without Wings

The moves that Lipizzans first learned for the battlefield are now part of classical dressage. The Spanish Riding School puts on world-famous classical dressage shows in Vienna.

Groups called troupes also put on classical dressage shows. Troupes travel from place to place for performances. Their shows are similar to those of the Spanish Riding School.

Strength and athletic ability make Lipizzans great classical dressage performers. Lipizzans perform with the grace of an Olympic gymnast. Their leaping ability and balance is unmatched by any other horse breed.

Learn about:
★ The quadrille
★ The levade
★ Classical dressage training

The Spanish Riding School puts on the most famous classical dressage performances.

Groups that perform classical dressage use Lipizzan stallions. Stallions are strong enough to do the most difficult maneuvers. The mares are used only for breeding.

Dancing to Music

When music blares out at classical dressage shows, Lipizzans are sure to have the audience's full attention. Lipizzans have a natural sense of rhythm. They step high in perfect time to the music.

In the quadrille, several horses do patterns to music. The horses move in a close formation, much like a unit of soldiers. They face each other and form lines and circles.

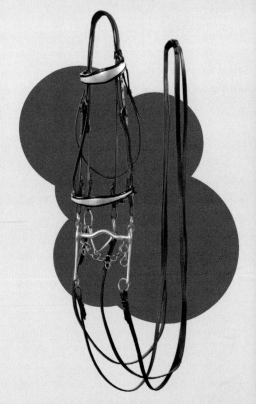

Other moves performed to music are the piaffe and the pirouette. Lipizzans trot in place to do the piaffe. They balance on their hind legs and pivot around in a circle for the pirouette.

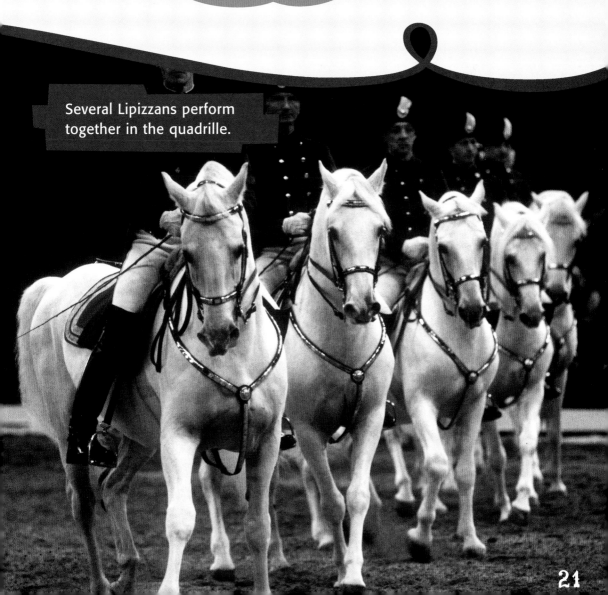

FACT

Dressage is a popular competitive sport. At competitions, horses and riders complete pattern tests. Competitors with the best scores win awards. They also can advance through dressage levels by passing the tests.

Several Lipizzans perform together in the quadrille.

Airs above the Ground

Only the strongest and most athletic stallions perform the advanced maneuvers called airs above the ground. In the capriole, the horse leaps high

Lipizzans leap high into the air to perform the capriole.

into the air and kicks out its back legs. The croupade is similar to the capriole. In this move, the horse leaps into the air while keeping its front and back legs tucked under its body.

To perform the courbette, the horse balances on its hind legs. It then jumps forward while keeping its front legs off the ground.

Lipizzans show their excellent balance in the levade. The horse stands on its hind legs for several seconds. The horse and rider are so still that they look like a statue.

Training

Lipizzans develop slowly. Other breeds like Thoroughbreds and Quarter Horses are strong enough to be ridden when they are 2 years old. Lipizzans usually aren't ridden until they are at least 3 ½ or 4 years old.

Classical dressage horses train for many years. At first, they learn to do maneuvers without a rider. Horses that do the airs above the ground train at least two years longer than other Lipizzans.

Chapter 4

Lipizzans in Action

North Americans who want to see a classical dressage show don't have to travel far. Occasionally, the Spanish Riding School puts on shows in the United States and other countries. The World Famous Lipizzaner troupe in Florida travels throughout North America. Other Lipizzan troupes that perform in the United States are Tempel Lipizzans and Herrmann's Original Royal Lipizzans.

Many Uses

Classical dressage is only one of the Lipizzan's talents. Powerful hindquarters help Lipizzans soar over tall jumps.

Learn about:
★ **North American troupes**
★ **Vaulting**
★ **Lipizzan care**

Some Lipizzans compete in jumping events.

▲ Lipizzans are reliable on trails.

Lipizzans also are good trail riding horses. They are steady and dependable even on the roughest ground.

Many people use Lipizzans as harness horses. Harness horses wear a set of leather straps. The straps connect the horses to a cart, wagon, carriage, or other vehicle. At Disneyland in Anaheim, California, Lipizzans pull carriages in parades.

The Lipizzan's wide back and steady trot make it a good horse for vaulting. Vaulting is a sport that combines gymnastics with horses. The horse is connected to a rope called a longe line. A person holds the longe line while the horse moves in circles. Gymnasts then do stunts on the horse's back.

Owning a Lipizzan

At the farm in Lipizza, strong winds blew in from the nearby sea. Lipizzans spent most of their time outside on the pasture's rough, rocky ground. These tough living conditions helped make today's Lipizzans hardy. Lipizzans usually stay healthy and strong on less food than most other horses do. But Lipizzans still need good care. They need food and water every day. Lipizzans also need shelter and exercise.

The number of Lipizzans in North America is small when compared to many other horse breeds. But the Lipizzan's popularity continues to grow. For each new owner, the rich history of the Lipizzan comes to life. When riding a Lipizzan, it is easy to imagine being a knight of the past, proudly marching a horse into battle.

Fast Facts:
The Lipizzan Horse

Name: The Lipizzan name comes from the town of Lipizza. Many of the first Lipizzans were bred there. Lipizza was once part of Austria. It is now in the country of Slovenia.

History: In 1562, the emperor of Austria started a horse farm. He bred Spanish horses with Karst horses at the farm. The mix created strong horses that were useful in wars. These horses became known as Lipizzans. Later, Arabians and Neapolitans were bred with Lipizzans.

Height: Lipizzans are 14.2 to 15.3 hands (about 5 feet or 1.5 meters) tall at the withers. Each hand equals 4 inches (10 centimeters).

Weight: 1,000 to 1,300 pounds (450 to 590 kilograms)

Colors: Almost all Lipizzans are gray.

Features: sturdy, muscular body; wide back and chest; strong shoulders and hindquarters; small ears; arched neck; long, flowing mane and tail; large eyes

Personality: intelligent, cooperative, gentle, calm

Abilities: Lipizzans are known as classical dressage horses. They also are popular harness horses.

Life span: 30 to 35 years

Glossary

capriole (KA-pree-ole)—a classical dressage move in which the horse leaps into the air and kicks out its back legs

dressage (druh-SAHJ)—a riding style in which horses complete a pattern while doing advanced moves; dressage riders use slight signals to guide their horses.

gymnastics (jim-NASS-tiks)—physical exercises that involve difficult and carefully controlled body movements

piaffe (pee-AHF)—a dressage move in which the horse trots in place

pirouette (puhr-uh-WET)—a classical dressage move in which the horse stands up on its hind legs and pivots in a circle

pivot (PIV-uht)—to turn while keeping at least one foot in place

quadrille (kwah-DRIL)—a performance involving several horses doing routines to music

stallion (STAL-yuhn)—an adult male horse that can be used for breeding

troupe (TROOP)—a group that travels to do performances

Read More

Bolté, Betty. *Dressage.* The Horse Library. Philadelphia: Chelsea House, 2002.

Ransford, Sandy. *Horse and Pony Breeds.* Kingfisher Riding Club. Boston: Kingfisher, 2003.

Stone, Lynn M. *Lipizzans.* Read all About Horses. Vero Beach, Fla.: Rourke, 1998.

Internet Sites

FactHound offers a safe, fun way to find Internet sites related to this book. All of the sites on FactHound have been researched by our staff.

Here's how:

1. Visit *www.facthound.com*
2. Type in this special code **0736854592** for age-appropriate sites. Or enter a search word related to this book for a more general search.
3. Click on the **Fetch It** button.

FactHound will fetch the best sites for you!

Index